31 Days of

Letting Go

*A Prayer Journey
to Freedom*

Michele Ellison & Lori Bremner

31 Days of Letting Go: A Prayer Journey to Freedom
Copyright © 2014 by Michele Ellison & Lori Bremner

All rights reserved. No part of this publication may be reproduced or transmitted without prior written permission from the author unless it is for the purpose of sharing the gospel message of Jesus Christ and advancing the Kingdom of God and is being shared free of charge.

ISBN-13:978-1496000477
ISBN-10:1496000471

Scripture quotations marked AMP are taken from the Amplified® Bible Copyright © 1954, 1958, 1962, 1964, 1965, 1987 by The Lockman Foundation Used by permission." (www.Lockman.org)

Scripture quotations marked HCSB are taken from the Holman Christian Standard Bible®, Copyright © 1999, 2000, 2002, 2003, 2009 by Holman Bible Publishers. Used by permission. Holman Christian Standard Bible®, Holman CSB®, and HCSB® are federally registered trademarks of Holman Bible Publishers.

Scripture quotations marked NASB are taken from the New American Standard Bible®, Copyright © 1960, 1962, 1963, 1968, 1971, 1972, 1973, 1975, 1977, 1995 by The Lockman Foundation Used by permission." (www.Lockman.org)

Scripture quotations marked NIV are taken from THE HOLY BIBLE, NEW INTERNATIONAL VERSION®, NIV® Copyright © 1973, 1978, 1984, 2011 by Biblica, Inc.® Used by permission. All rights reserved worldwide.

Contents

INTRODUCTION	**4**
DAY 1	**9**
DAY 2	**10**
DAY 3	**11**
DAY 4	**12**
DAY 5	**13**
DAY 6	**14**
DAY 7	**15**
DAY 8	**18**
DAY 9	**19**
DAY 10	**20**
DAY 11	**21**
DAY 12	**22**
DAY 13	**23**
DAY 14	**24**
DAY 15	**27**
DAY 16	**28**
DAY 17	**29**
DAY 18	**30**
DAY 19	**31**
DAY 20	**32**
DAY 21	**33**
DAY 22	**36**
DAY 23	**37**
DAY 24	**38**
DAY 25	**39**
DAY 26	**40**
DAY 27	**41**
DAY 28	**42**
DAY 29	**45**
DAY 30	**46**
DAY 31	**47**
PRAYERS	**50**

Introduction

Introduction

This book, *31 Days of Letting Go*, began with our annual women's retreat. The theme of the weekend was "Letting Go and Letting God" and in the months leading up to the actual retreat, we knew God was going to do something big. We were praying for a huge impact on each woman's life, for genuine change, for freedom to live and walk in the spiritually abundant life God intended. We met one day at Lori's house, Bibles and hearts open to whatever God wanted. Then each day for the next 31 days, we emailed one prayer a day to everyone registered for the retreat. And what God has done is simply amazing!

The retreat itself was powerful, lives were changed, prayers were answered in special and incredible ways. When we returned home, energized and recharged, we had many requests to continue sending the prayers. So we began the Facebook page, 31 Days of Letting Go, (www.facebook.com/31daysoflettinggo), which has grown to over 150,000 people praying the Word of God and seeking His power for freedom and victory! Praise God!!

Not long ago, God placed a desire in Lori's heart to put the prayers into book format about the same time God was placing a desire on Michele's heart to write a book! God lines everything up perfectly and His plan is always exciting!

After much prayer and seeking God's direction, we moved forward and the prayer book you are now reading was born. We have heard so many stories of how God has used these Scripture verses and prayers to change lives. We would love to hear from you too! If you have a testimony or story to share, or just want to connect, join us on the Facebook page. We would be so blessed and delighted to hear how God is using His Word in your life.

Thank you, dear sister (or brother), in Christ for choosing this book. We agree with you in prayer for strength, freedom, and victory in Jesus' name. May you grow closer to Jesus through every prayer and every page, and may God bless you abundantly with freedom as you let go, trust Him…and never look back!

Much Love,

Michele & Lori

Now to Him who is able to do above and beyond all that we ask or think according to the power that works in us—to Him be glory in the church and in Christ Jesus to all generations, forever and ever. Amen (Ephesians 3:20-21, HCSB)

Are You Ready?

You are about to begin an exciting journey that will transform you as you move toward the abundant life Christ offers. As you begin to let go of the strongholds and lies of this world to grab hold of God's truth, you will find complete freedom at the feet of Jesus. But first, you have an important question to ponder, one only you can answer, one that is crucial for your success in finding freedom…Do you know Jesus? Is He your Savior?

If you've accepted Jesus, we rejoice with you in excitement and anticipation for what God is going to do in the days ahead. He has a great plan for you and wants to use you for His Glory. Get ready!

If you don't yet know Jesus, we rejoice with you too even more because right now, this very moment, is the perfect opportunity to meet Him! He loves you and is offering you the gift of eternity with Him. This gift also comes with perfect peace, joy and abundant life. As you seek freedom from whatever has you in bondage, seek the One with the strength to free you! He has already overcome the world and He loves you. He is ready to offer you new life, one of fulfillment and purpose empowered to overcome and equipped for amazing things. I so hope and pray you will accept it!

It is one of the simplest and yet most challenging, exciting things you will ever do—God's Word tells us that, "If you confess with your mouth, "Jesus is Lord," and believe in your heart that God raised Him from the dead, you will be saved." (Romans 10:9, HCSB). It's not hard…but it will change everything! And if you're not quite ready, that's okay too. Join us on this journey and I pray before it's over, you have found the peace and love of Christ.

~*~

We want to challenge you over the next 31 days to use these prayers as a starting point to begin an exciting time of worship, prayer, and intimate fellowship with the God of the universe. Begin by asking God for a willing heart, eyes to see, and ears to hear exactly what He has for you. I pray this is just the beginning of an exciting journey of freedom, power, peace, and joy that transforms you into the image of Jesus!

So take a deep breath, get ready to let go of every sin and ask God to do a mighty work of transformation in you! We are praying for you and asking God to renew you each day! When you reach the end of this 31-day journey, we pray you are walking in daily freedom, peace, and joy knowing how loved you truly are!

And this journey never has to end! When you finish your first 31 days, start over at the beginning asking God to reveal His next fresh work of transformation and freedom in your life!

***

Therefore, since we also have such a large cloud of witnesses surrounding us, let us lay aside every weight and the sin that so easily ensnares us. Let us run with endurance the race that lies before us, keeping our eyes on Jesus, the source and perfecter of our faith, who for the joy that lay before Him endured a cross and despised the shame and has sat down at the right hand of God's throne
(Hebrews 12:1-3, HCSB).

Therefore, since we also have such a large cloud of witnesses surrounding us, let us lay aside every weight and the sin that so easily ensnares us. Let us run with endurance the race that lies before us, keeping our eyes on Jesus, the source and perfecter of our faith, who for the joy that lay before Him endured a cross and despised the shame and has sat down at the right hand of God's throne. (Hebrews 12:1-3, HCSB)

On Your Mark...

As you plant your feet on the starting line and prepare to begin this journey, spend some time preparing your heart for the days ahead. Ask God for wisdom and strength to start strong and finish well. Ask God to do a genuine, long-lasting transformation in you that will renew you, refresh you, and equip you for life.

Over the next 31 days you may want to keep a journal to record your thoughts, prayers and any special Scripture verses you want to commit to memory. This will also be a treasured place to note how God is transforming you as you move toward perfect peace and complete freedom in Christ.

Get Set...

This journey will be difficult, but more importantly, this journey will be rewarding above anything we can even imagine! And never forget --you are not alone. We have all believed lies and been imprisoned by them... my struggle may be a little different than yours, but sister, we all have a struggle!

We all have a very real enemy prowling around like a lion to see which one of us he can devour first. Beloved, we must stand strong on the Word of God, armed with His truth, so we can not only defeat the enemy, we can rise higher and higher to the life God intends for us--a life of victory and freedom!

Jesus offers us abundant life for the taking so let's begin our journey to freedom! It will not be easy and there will be days we feel like giving up, but if we persevere to the end, we will reap a harvest! (Galatians 6:9). Our victory will be all the sweeter having been earned through an ever-deepening love of Scripture and closeness with God. Are you ready? I know I am! So...

Go!

The following verses and prayers are for you. Make sure you spend time reading the verses and letting the truth of God's Word seep deep into your soul, then use the prayers to cry out to God and make them your own. Words on a page will not change you, but the Holy Spirit can completely transform you and make you new if you will let Him!

Use the prayers as a starting point to let go of every lie as you draw closer to God and let His power and might bring you to complete victory... I am praying for you, and I am so proud of you. Never give up seeking God and running toward His love, grace, and transforming mercy!

It's time to let go of every lie and knock down every stronghold and grab hold of the abundant life that is ours in Christ Jesus!
What lies are you holding onto? What deceptive thinking has crept in and replaced the truth of God in your life? What is it that you need freedom from?

It's time to let go!

Week One

*"Look, I am about to do something new;
even now it is coming. Do you not see it?
Indeed, I will make a way in the wilderness,
rivers in the desert."*
(Isaiah 43:19, HCSB)

Day 1

Scripture Focus

"For though we live in the world, we do not wage war as the world does. The weapons we fight with are not the weapons of the world. On the contrary, they have divine power to demolish strongholds. We demolish arguments and every pretension that sets itself up against the knowledge of God, and we take captive every thought to make it obedient to Christ."
(2 Corinthians 10:3-5, NIV)

Pray

Lord, You desire for me to live in freedom. You never intended for me to live in bondage or fear. Thank You for giving me the weapons I need for victory; weapons with divine power to demolish strongholds. Lord, destroy arguments and every bit of pride that keeps me from knowing You more. Take my every thought captive and make it obedient to Christ. (2 Cor. 10:3-5)

Reflect

What am I afraid of?
What am I in bondage to?
What changes do I need to make today?

Day 2

Scripture Focus

"Yours, O LORD, is the greatness and the power and the glory and the victory and the majesty, indeed everything that is in the heavens and the earth; Yours is the dominion, O LORD, and You exalt Yourself as head over all. Both riches and honor come from You, and You rule over all, and in Your hand is power and might; and it lies in Your hand to make great and to strengthen everyone."
(1 Chronicles 29:11-12, NASB)

Pray

Father, I acknowledge that You are the Lord Almighty. You are the first, You are the last, and apart from You there is no other God. Make me witness to the fact that there is no other rock but You. Enable me to say with full assurance, "I know not one." (Isa. 44:6) Help me overcome the stronghold of idolatry and to acknowledge Your sovereignty and greatness in every area of my life.

Reflect

What have I placed above God in my life?
What areas of life do I need to surrender control to God?
How can I offer praise and thanks for God's greatness and power?

_____
_____
_____
_____
_____
_____
_____

Day 3

Scripture Focus

"Therefore if you have any encouragement from being united with Christ, if any comfort from his love, if any common sharing in the Spirit, if any tenderness and compassion, then make my joy complete by being like-minded, having the same love, being one in spirit and of one mind. Do nothing out of selfish ambition or vain conceit. Rather, in humility value others above yourselves," (Philippians 2:1-3, NIV)

Pray

Lord, help me do nothing out of selfish ambition or vain conceit. Help me in humility to consider others better than myself. (Philippians 2:3) Reveal to me anything You disapprove of; bring it to my attention and help me to be an overcomer!

Reflect

How do I consider others better than myself?
How do I win victory over my struggles?
What changes do I need to make?

Day 4

Scripture Focus

"Behold, You desire truth in the inner being; make me therefore to know wisdom in my inmost heart." (Psalm 51:6, AMP); "They exchanged the truth about God for a lie, and worshiped and served created things rather than the Creator—who is forever praised. Amen." (Romans 1:25, NIV)

Pray

Lord God, You desire truth and sincerity. Fill my mind with Your wisdom. (Ps. 51:6). Teach me to discern Your truth, and may I never exchange it for a lie (Rom. 1:25). Reveal the lies I've believed for so long. Help me recognize them and replace them with Your truth. Lord, set me free.

Reflect

What lies have I believed?
What does God's Word say?
How do I protect myself from believing lies in the future?

Day 5

Scripture Focus

"As for what was sown among thorns, this is he who hears the Word, but the cares of the world and the pleasure *and* delight *and* glamour *and* deceitfulness of riches choke *and* suffocate the Word, and it yields no fruit. As for what was sown on good soil, this is he who hears the Word and grasps *and* comprehends it; he indeed bears fruit and yields in one case a hundred times as much as was sown, in another sixty times as much, and in another thirty."
(Matthew 13:22-23, AMP)

Pray

Father, may Your Holy Word never be choked out by the worries of this life, the deceitfulness of wealth, or desires for other things, (Mark 4:19). Give me a desire to spend more time with You in Your Word than with the distractions of this life. Help me read and study Your Word, growing closer to You, the Author, rather than just rely on Christian books and other sources.

Reflect

What is choking out the Word of God from my life?
How can I spend more time in the Word of God?
What does it mean to bear fruit?

_____
_____
_____
_____
_____
_____
_____
_____

Day 6

Scripture Focus

"These things I have spoken to you, so that in Me you may have peace. In the world you have tribulation, but take courage; I have overcome the world." (John 16:33, NASB); "Yet amid all these things we are more than conquerors *and* gain a surpassing victory through Him Who loved us." (Romans 8:37, AMP)

Pray

Lord, Your Word tells me I will have trouble in this world, (John 16:33), but You also assure me that I don't have to live in defeat. In You, I can have peace, freedom, and victory. Help me turn to You first and be filled with Your strength. Help me live with Your power. No matter my struggle, help me remember that You have overcome the world, You love me, and, in You, I am more than a conqueror! (Romans 8:37).

Reflect

How do I grow stronger?
How do I live in daily victory?
What does it mean to have peace?

Day 7

Scripture Focus

"Before this faith came, we were confined under the law, imprisoned until the coming faith was revealed. (Galatians 3:23, HSCB); Therefore if any person is [ingrafted] in Christ (the Messiah) he is a new creation (a new creature altogether); the old [previous moral and spiritual condition] has passed away. Behold, the fresh *and* new has come!" (2 Corinthians 5:17, AMP)

Pray

Father, thank You for the faith You have given me. Before this faith came, I was held prisoner by the law, locked up until faith was revealed. (Gal. 3:23) But now Lord, in You, I am a new creation. The old has gone and I am free. Help me walk in this freedom every day with renewed strength and joy. (2 Cor. 5:17)

Reflect

What has God set me free from?
What still holds me captive?
How can I walk in complete freedom every day?

_____
_____
_____
_____
_____
_____
_____
_____
_____
_____

Congratulations! I am so proud of you for finishing Week One! I hope and pray that God is revealing the lies and strongholds He would have you let go of and leading you to a place of wonderful freedom. I also hope you are enjoying a deeper walk and feeling an increased measure of the presence of God in your everyday life. That is my prayer for you, and I so hope it is being answered in a powerful way!

As you begin week two, take a quiet moment to pause and reflect over the last week and make a note of everything that God has been teaching you or revealing to you. How is your time in prayer and His word beginning to change you? How is God growing your faith and your trust in Him? What special blessings has He surprised you with? Write them below.

_____
_____
_____
_____
_____
_____
_____
_____
_____
_____
_____
_____
_____
_____
_____

Week Two

"but you will receive power when the Holy Spirit has come upon you; and you shall be My witnesses both in Jerusalem, and in all Judea and Samaria, and even to the remotest part of the earth."
(Acts 1:8, NASB)

Day 8

Scripture Focus

"For whatever is born of God overcomes the world; and this is the victory that has overcome the world—our faith. Who is the one who overcomes the world, but he who believes that Jesus is the Son of God?" (I John 5:4-5, NASB); "Immediately the boy's father cried out and said, 'I do believe; help my unbelief.'"
(Mark 9:24, NASB)

Pray

Lord, according to Your Holy Word, my faith in You and my belief that Jesus is the Son of God gives me victory over the world. (I John 5:4-5) Help me believe You and let me see that faith is crucial if I am going to be a victor and an overcomer. Lord, please increase my faith in You and help my unbelief. (Mark 9:24)

Reflect

Have I truly been born of God?
How does my faith in God give me victory?
What areas of my faith are weak in unbelief?

_____
_____
_____
_____
_____
_____
_____
_____

Day 9

Scripture Focus

"He feeds on ashes; a deceived heart has turned him aside. And he cannot deliver himself, nor say, 'Is there not a lie in my right hand?' (Isaiah 44:20, NASB); "and you will know the truth, and the truth will make you free." (John 8:32, NASB)

Pray

Father, I acknowledge that at times in my life I have fed on ashes instead of Your Word. I have let my misguided heart lead me astray. Help me recognize when I am holding onto a lie and trusting a powerless idol for my security, (Isaiah 44:20). Teach me to walk in Your truth and to completely trust in You alone.

Reflect

What lies have I believed?
How do I trust God for my security?
What do I need to surrender to God?

Day 10

Scripture Focus

"For the word of God is alive and active. Sharper than any double-edged sword, it penetrates even to dividing soul and spirit, joints and marrow; it judges the thoughts and attitudes of the heart. Nothing in all creation is hidden from God's sight. Everything is uncovered and laid bare before the eyes of him to whom we must give account." (Hebrews 4:12-13, NIV); "She is clothed with strength and dignity; she can laugh at the days to come." (Proverbs 31:25, NIV). "Create in me a clean heart, O God, and renew a right and steadfast spirit within me." (Psalm 51:10, AMP).

Pray

LORD, I praise You and magnify Your powerful name! Your Word is alive, powerful, and active. Sharper than any double-edged sword, it penetrates even to dividing soul and spirit, joints and marrow; it judges the thoughts and attitudes of my heart. You see me, You know me, and I am laid bare before You. Your Word exposes me for who I really am. (Heb. 4:12-13) Transform me, Lord. Clothe me in strength and dignity. Create in me a clean heart, and renew a steadfast spirit within me, (Psalm 51:10).

Reflect

What am I trying to hide even from God?
How do I feel knowing I am completely laid bare before God?
What does it mean to be clothed in dignity and strength?

_____
_____
_____
_____
_____

Day 11

Scripture Focus

"I will give thanks to You, for I am fearfully and wonderfully made; Wonderful are Your works, And my soul knows it very well." (Psalm 139:14, NASB)

Pray

O Lord, please forgive me for my doubts. You are greater than my insecurities, and stronger than my fears. Help me to praise You because I am fearfully and wonderfully made; Your works are wonderful, I know that full well, (Psalm 139:14). Help me trust You completely as I will walk in Your freedom, (Psalm 119:45).

Reflect

Do I know I am loved and cherished by God?
How does God show me His love daily?
How can I show my love and thankfulness to God daily?

Day 12

Scripture Focus

"Set your minds on things above, not on earthly things." (Colossians. 3:2, NIV); "fixing our eyes on Jesus, the author and perfecter of faith, who for the joy set before Him endured the cross, despising the shame, and has sat down at the right hand of the throne of God." (Hebrews 12:2, NASB)

Pray

Lord, help me set my mind on things above, not on earthly things. (Col. 3:2) Help me allow Your Spirit to teach me to separate the temporary from the eternal and to set my focus on You (2 Cor. 4:18).

Reflect

How does worry defeat me?
What do I place above God in my daily life?
What happens when I move my thoughts to God?

_____
_____
_____
_____
_____
_____
_____
_____
_____
_____

Day 13

Scripture Focus

"Search me, God, and know my heart; test me and know my anxious thoughts. See if there is any offensive way in me, and lead me in the way everlasting." (Psalm 139:23-24, NIV)

Pray

Search my heart and mind, O God. Know my heart; test me and know my anxious thoughts. Lord, find every offensive way in me, and replace it with Your Truth. Lead me in the way everlasting (Ps. 139:23-24) and walking in Your freedom.

Reflect

What am I anxious about?
Can I trust God with my thoughts?
How can I spend more quiet time with God?

_____
_____
_____
_____
_____
_____
_____
_____
_____
_____
_____
_____
_____

Day 14

Scripture Focus

"But if the Spirit of Him who raised Jesus from the dead dwells in you, He who raised Christ Jesus from the dead will also give life to your mortal bodies through His Spirit who dwells in you." (Romans. 8:11, NASB); "But he said to me, 'My grace is sufficient for you, for my power is made perfect in weakness.' Therefore I will boast all the more gladly about my weaknesses, so that Christ's power may rest on me." (2 Corinthians 12:9, NIV)

Pray

Lord Jesus, You are alive! Thank You for conquering death and saving me. The same power that raised You from the dead lives in me. (Rom. 8:11) Fill me with Your Holy Spirit Lord and teach me to walk in Your ways. Your grace is sufficient and in my weakness You are strong. O Lord, may Your power rest in me! (2 Cor. 12:9)

Reflect

Am I allowing the Holy Spirit to renew me daily?
How is the work of the Holy Spirit evident in my life?
How do I depend on His strength in my weakness?

_____
_____
_____
_____
_____
_____
_____
_____

We are halfway finished, and I so dearly hope and pray that God is doing something miraculous in your life. You are so loved and cherished by the Creator of the universe, and He is delighted in you as you seek to know Him more! You are beautiful and I hope your burdens are significantly lighter as you are letting go of the lies and negative thoughts and emotions, and growing deeper and deeper in your relationship with God.

Before you move on to week three, please take a few quiet moments to pause and reflect over the past week, asking the Holy Spirit to reveal to you what He is doing in you and through you, and then make a note of any blessings or thoughts below. I am praying for you to persevere and finish strong…and asking God to bless you abundantly!

_____
_____
_____
_____
_____
_____
_____
_____
_____
_____
_____
_____
_____
_____
_____
_____
_____

Week Three

*"Therefore, if anyone is in Christ,
he is a new creation;
old things have passed away,
and look, new things have come."*
(2 Corinthians 5:17, HCSB)

Day 15

Scripture Focus

"During the days of Jesus' life on earth, he offered up prayers and petitions with fervent cries and tears to the one who could save him from death, and he was heard because of his reverent submission." (Hebrews 5:7, NIV); "pray without ceasing;" (1 Thess 5:17, NASB)

Pray

Father, even Jesus prayed to You for help while He lived on earth. He spent quiet time with You and prayed with loud cries and tears. (Heb. 5:7) Teach me to pray and seek You for help. Teach me to lean on Your strength and power. Lord, help me to pray, hear my prayers, and teach me to trust You completely.

Reflect

What does it mean to pray without ceasing?
How do I learn to trust God completely?
Do I value my time with God and protect it?

Day 16

Scripture Focus

"… And all of you clothe yourselves with humility toward one another, because God resists the proud but gives grace to the humble." (I Peter 5:5, HCSB)

Pray

Father, You resist the proud but give grace to the humble. Help me clothe myself with humility toward others (1 Pet. 5:5), considering others above myself, (Phil. 2:3). I need Your grace every moment of every day. Protect me from every form of pride and help me maintain a humble, compassionate heart.

Reflect

In what ways do I struggle with pride?
Does my pride prevent me from truly loving others?
Am I guilty of false humility?

Day 17

Scripture Focus

"Everything is permissible for me,' but not everything is helpful. 'Everything is permissible for me,' but I will not be brought under the control of anything." (1 Cor. 6:12, HCSB); "So whether you eat or drink or whatever you do, do it all for the glory of God." (1 Cor. 10:31, NIV)

Pray

Lord, God, You are my first desire and worthy of all praise. In all I do and say, help me make healthy, wholesome choices that honor You and bring You glory, (Col. 3:17). Free me from bondage to any questionable habits or hobbies. May I never allow worldly things to have control over me (1 Cor. 6:12). Rather, I choose to submit to You alone and experience freedom as I am guided and led by Your Spirit, (Gal. 5:18).

Reflect

What have I allowed to control me?
What areas of my life do not give glory to God?
What do I gain by giving God control?

Day 18

Scripture Focus

"But you, dear friends, as you build yourselves up in your most holy faith and pray in the Holy Spirit, keep yourselves in the love of God, expecting the mercy of our Lord Jesus Christ for eternal life. Have mercy on those who doubt; save others by snatching them from the fire; have mercy on others but with fear, hating even the garment defiled by the flesh. Now to Him who is able to protect you from stumbling and to make you stand in the presence of His glory, blameless and with great joy, to the only God our Savior, through Jesus Christ our Lord, be glory, majesty, power, and authority before all time, now and forever. Amen."
(Jude 20-25, HCSB)

Pray

Lord, You are my God who strengthens me, helps me, and upholds me in victory, power, and salvation. (Isaiah 41:10). Teach me to listen to You and accept Your perfect love. Help me have Your great joy. You are the only God, the One who saves me. To You be glory, greatness, power, and authority through Jesus Christ our Lord for all time past, present, and forever. Amen (Jude 24-25)

Reflect

What must I surrender to God today?
Do I completely accept God's perfect love for me?
Does God have complete authority in my life?

_____
_____
_____
_____
_____

Day 19

Scripture Focus

"Therefore, since we also have such a large cloud of witnesses surrounding us, let us lay aside every weight and the sin that so easily ensnares us. Let us run with endurance the race that lies before us, keeping our eyes on Jesus, the source and perfecter of our faith, who for the joy that lay before Him endured a cross and despised the shame and has sat down at the right hand of God's throne" (Hebrews 12:1-2, HCSB). "But You, O LORD, are a shield for me, my glory [and my honor], and the One who lifts my head" (Ps. 3:3 AMP)

Pray

Lord Jesus, You love me and have set me free, (Rom. 8:2). Reveal the lies I'm holding onto. Help me let go of the sin that so easily entangles me and holds me captive. Keep my focus on You, the author and perfecter of my faith (Heb. 12:2), the lifter of my head, and the One who has made me free.

Reflect

What am I easily entangled by?
What keeps me from letting go?
How does Jesus perfect my faith?

_____
_____
_____
_____
_____
_____
_____

Day 20

Scripture Focus

"Humble yourselves, therefore, under God's mighty hand, that he may lift you up in due time." (1 Peter 5:6, NIV); "For who is God besides the LORD? And who is the Rock except our God? It is God who arms me with strength and keeps my way secure." (Psalm 18:31-32, NIV)

Pray

Lord, help me overcome my pride. Help me be full of Your Spirit and not full of myself. Enable me to humble myself under Your mighty hand so You can lift me up in due time (I Pet. 5:6) You are always trustworthy, and Your timing is always right. Help me to humble myself now so that You are free to do wonders later.

Reflect

How does my humility bring freedom?
Why is pride an obstacle to my strength?
Where does my true strength come from?

Day 21

Scripture Focus

"Be strong and courageous, do not be afraid or tremble at them, for the LORD your God is the one who goes with you. He will not fail you or forsake you." (Deuteronomy 31:6, NASB); "Therefore let us draw near with confidence to the throne of grace, so that we may receive mercy and find grace to help in time of need."
(Hebrews 4:16, NASB)

Pray

Father God, make me strong and courageous. Help me never be afraid or intimidated because of anyone else. Help me live to please You rather than seeking the praises of men. For You, the Lord my God, are always with me. You will never leave me or forsake me. (Deut. 31:6)

Reflect

When am I most tempted to seek the praises of others?
How do humility and strength work together?
How do I live to please God?

Beautiful one, we are almost there…don't give up! Keep going and behold all that God has for you. No matter where we are in our faith, we can always grow deeper and closer to God. He is limitless and His love is endless!

I so wish we could sit down together and discuss what God is teaching you and freeing you from! I bet we share some of the same struggles and we definitely share the weight of carrying them for too long so I pray you are growing lighter and freer by the day! Take some quiet moments to reflect and rejoice and give thanks to God for all He is doing in you—and He isn't finished yet!

Week Four

*"Let us not become weary in doing good,
for at the proper time we will reap a harvest
if we do not give up."*
(Galatians 6:9, NIV)

Day 22

Scripture Focus

"I am the LORD, your Holy One, Israel's Creator, your King.' This is what the LORD says—he who made a way through the sea, a path through the mighty waters, "Forget the former things; do not dwell on the past. See, I am doing a new thing! Now it springs up; do you not perceive it? I am making a way in the wilderness and streams in the wasteland. The wild animals honor me, the jackals and the owls, because I provide water in the wilderness and streams in the wasteland, to give drink to my people, my chosen, the people I formed for myself that they may proclaim my praise." (Isaiah 43:15-16, 18-21, NIV)

Pray

Lord, my Holy One, my Creator, my King. You are the One who made a way through the sea, a path through the mighty waters. (Isa. 43:15-16) You alone are the Lord my God. Lord, I desire to love You. Help me listen to Your voice, and hold fast to You, for You, Lord, are my life, (Deut. 30:20), and in You, I am free.

Reflect

Am I clinging to my past?
What is God doing in me now?
List what God is doing and declare His praise!

_____
_____
_____
_____
_____
_____
_____

Day 23

Scripture Focus

"The Spirit of the Lord GOD is on Me, because the LORD has anointed Me to bring good news to the poor. He has sent Me to heal the brokenhearted, to proclaim liberty to the captives and freedom to the prisoners;" (Isaiah 61:1, HCSB)

Pray

Lord, You proclaim freedom for the captives. (Isaiah 61:1) I belong to You and I am no longer a slave to this world or it's fears- I am free! Help me to live in Your freedom daily and look to You for my confidence and strength.

Reflect

What fears hold me prisoner?
What philosophies of this world are holding me captive?
How do I live in the freedom Christ has proclaimed for me?

_____
_____
_____
_____
_____
_____
_____
_____
_____
_____
_____
_____

Day 24

Scripture Focus

"Create in me a pure heart, O God, and renew a steadfast spirit within me. Do not cast me from your presence or take your Holy Spirit from me. Restore to me the joy of your salvation and grant me a willing spirit, to sustain me." (Psalm 51:10-12, NIV) "Therefore, if anyone is in Christ, the new creation has come: The old has gone, the new is here!" (2 Cor. 5:17 NIV).

Pray

Lord, I need You and desire to Know You more. Remove every sinful thought, and create in me a pure heart and a steadfast spirit, (Ps. 51:10-12). The old is gone. Help me let go of shame, regret, and every sin, that I may live in Your freedom, as You desire for me. I am a brand new creation and I praise You! (Gal. 5:17).

Reflect

Am I loyal to God?
How am I renewed?
How does a willing spirit to obey God sustain me?

_____
_____
_____
_____
_____
_____
_____
_____
_____
_____

Day 25

Scripture Focus

"May the God of hope fill you with all joy and peace as you trust in him, so that you may overflow with hope by the power of the Holy Spirit." (Romans 15:13, NIV)

Pray

Lord, I believe Your Word, Your promises, and I need Your strength. I pray that You, the God of hope, will fill me with all joy and peace as I trust You. Help me abound in hope by the power of Your Holy Spirit (Rom. 15:13).

Reflect

What are the promises God has given me?
How do I surrender to the power of the Holy Spirit?
Where do I find my hope? My peace? My joy?

_____
_____
_____
_____
_____
_____
_____
_____
_____
_____
_____
_____
_____

Day 26

Scripture Focus

"See to it that no one takes you captive through philosophy and empty deception, according to the tradition of men, according to the elementary principles of the world, rather than according to Christ." (Colossians 2:8, NASB)

Pray

Father, teach me to abide in You and trust You completely. Strengthen me that I might never be taken captive by lies or philosophies of this world, or rely on human tradition (Col. 2:8) Help me trust completely in Your great strength, rely on Your Word above all else, and live by Your truth.

Reflect

How do I distinguish lies from truth?
How can I protect myself from believing lies?
What is empty deception?

Day 27

Scripture Focus

"And that is what some of you were. But you were washed, you were sanctified, you were justified in the name of the Lord Jesus Christ and by the Spirit of our God." (1 Cor. 6:11, NIV); "As the Father has loved me, so have I loved you. Now remain in my love." (John 15:9, NIV)

Pray

Dear God, no matter what I once was, I have been washed, I have been sanctified, and I have been justified in the name of the Lord Jesus Christ and by the Spirit of our God, (1 Cor. 6:11). I am clean, and I am free! Lord God, help me fully accept how much You love me, and help me abide in Your freedom and love (John 15:9).

Reflect

What is God setting me free from?
What choices do I need to make to remain free?
Do I accept that I am loved unconditionally?

_____
_____
_____
_____
_____
_____
_____
_____
_____
_____
_____

Day 28

Scripture Focus

"Cast all your anxiety on him because he cares for you" (1 Peter 5:7, NIV); "Do not be anxious about anything, but in every situation, by prayer and petition, with thanksgiving, present your requests to God. And the peace of God, which transcends all understanding, will guard your hearts and your minds in Christ Jesus" (Phil. 4:6-7, NIV)

Pray

Lord, teach me to turn all my worries and cares over to You, (1 Peter 5:7). Remove every fear, anxiety, and sinful desire, and fill me with Your peace beyond what I can comprehend. Guard my heart and my mind in Christ Jesus (Phil. 4:5-7) and help me abide in Your love and grace.

Reflect

What am I worried about?
Do I trust God to handle it?
How do I let God guard my heart and my mind?

_____
_____
_____
_____
_____
_____
_____
_____
_____

We are almost finished, sweet sister, and I pray that God is doing such an amazing transformation in you! These last few days that are left are the perfect time to let go of whatever is still weighing you down. What is it that you are still clinging to? I pray you let it go to be filled with the most incredible, overwhelming peace and strength as you do! Be so completely full of Jesus there is no room for lies!

God has such an amazing plan for you! He loves you with an unconditional love and desires You completely. He knew you and loved you before you were born, and has prepared a beautiful path for you. Follow after Him and seek Him, and as you let go of these lies, never let go of Him!

As you hold tightly to Him, He is holding you even tighter and He will never let you go! Give Him thanks and praise!

_____
_____
_____
_____
_____
_____
_____
_____
_____
_____
_____
_____
_____

Week Five

> "So if the Son sets you free,
> you will be free indeed."
> *(John 8:36, NIV)*

Day 29

Scripture Focus

"The LORD is my rock and my fortress and my deliverer; My God, my rock, in whom I take refuge, My shield and the horn of my salvation, my stronghold and my refuge; 'For who is God, besides the LORD? And who is a rock, besides our God? God is my strong fortress; And He sets the blameless in His way."
(2 Samuel 22:2-3a, 32-33, NASB)

Pray

You, O Lord, are my rock, my refuge, my stronghold, and my deliverer! (2 Samuel 22:2). Remove every evil thing I have exalted above You and help me rest in the knowledge that You and You alone are my greatest stronghold! I am not held captive any longer. In Christ, I am free. In my freedom, help me make choices that bring You glory, Lord, and which bring me closer to You. Increase my knowledge of You and my desire to walk in Your freedom!

Reflect

What do I need to let go of?
How can God help me?
Do I live as if God is my greatest stronghold?

_____
_____
_____
_____
_____
_____
_____
_____

Day 30

Scripture Focus

"Do not conform to the pattern of this world, but be transformed by the renewing of your mind. Then you will be able to test and approve what God's will is—his good, pleasing and perfect will" (Romans 12:2, NIV).

Pray

Almighty God, help me no longer conform to the pattern of this world, but transform me by the renewing of my mind. Lord, help me place my life before You as an offering. Change me from the inside out. Help me stand firm against the sins of the culture, and help me look like Jesus as You develop well-formed maturity in me (Romans 12:1-2).

Reflect

What is the pattern of this world?
How am I transformed and renewed to maturity?
What behaviors and thoughts are hindering my growth in Christ?

_____
_____
_____
_____
_____
_____
_____
_____
_____
_____

Day 31

Scripture Focus

"Therefore, there is now no condemnation for those who are in Christ Jesus, because through Christ Jesus the law of the Spirit who gives life has set you free from the law of sin and death." (Romans 8:1-2, NIV); "It is for freedom that Christ has set us free. Stand firm, then, and do not let yourselves be burdened again by a yoke of slavery" (Galatians 5:1, NIV); "I am able to do all things through Him who strengthens me." (Philippians 4:13, HCSB)

Pray

Father, Your Word says that it is for freedom that Christ has set me free. With all my heart, I desire to stand firm and never again allow myself to be burdened by a yoke of slavery (Gal. 5:1). I surrender and submit to You completely, and rest in Your goodness and strength. I acknowledge my weakness and rejoice because I know that Your power is made perfect in my weakness (2 Cor. 12:9-10). Strengthen me to walk in the freedom You have already given me. Teach me to stand firm. I can do all things in Christ who strengthens me! (Phil. 4:13)

Reflect

How do I stand firm?
What freedom do I have in Christ?
What is holding me back from an empowered life of freedom in Christ?

_____

_____

_____

_____

_____

This has been an emotional and challenging journey, but I pray it has overflowed with blessing and victory and that we are all very different than when we began!

God has begun a work in each of us that can and should continue into eternity—the journey of knowing Him more and clinging to His truth. Hold so tightly to Him and His glorious truth that there is no room for lies…never again will we trade our feast for ashes—He is making us radiant! And I pray the work He is doing in you is simply too good to keep to yourself—I pray you shout from the rooftops "How Great is Our God!"

Much love and abundant blessings to you sweet friend and I pray you stand strong and remain free to God's glory!

No, in all these things we are more than conquerors through him who loved us. For I am convinced that neither death nor life, neither angels nor demons, neither the present nor the future, nor any powers, neither height nor depth, nor anything else in all creation, will be able to separate us from the love of God that is in Christ Jesus our Lord. (Romans 8:37-39, NIV)

The following pages contain the daily prayers of our journey. Continue to pray them each day asking God to bring freedom in every area of your life. Copy them onto note cards and post them in your car, on the fridge, wherever you will see them as a reminder to seek God first and continually cry out to Him for every need and every desire.

If you don't already, we invite you to follow our Facebook page, 31 Days of Letting Go, where we post the prayers each day.

This journey of letting go of lies and grabbing hold of God's truth should never end! Continue seeking God and be amazed not only at what He can do… but Who He is!

Keep Praying!

31 Days of Letting Go

Day 1- Lord, You desire for me to live in freedom. You never intended for me to live in bondage or fear. Thank You for giving me the weapons I need for victory; weapons with divine power to demolish strongholds. Lord, destroy arguments and every bit of pride that keeps me from knowing You more. Take my every thought captive and make it obedient to Christ. (2 Cor. 10:3-5)

Day 2- Father, I acknowledge that You are the Lord Almighty. You are the first, You are the last, and apart from You there is no other God. Make me witness to the fact that there is no other rock but You. Enable me to say with full assurance, "I know not one." (Isa. 44:6) Help me overcome the stronghold of idolatry and to acknowledge Your sovereignty and greatness in every area of my life.

Day 3- Lord, help me do nothing out of selfish ambition or vain conceit. Help me in humility to consider others better than myself. (Philippians 2:3) Reveal to me anything You disapprove of; bring it to my attention and help me to be an overcomer!

Day 4- Lord God, You desire truth and sincerity. Fill my mind with Your wisdom. (Ps. 51:6). Teach me to discern Your truth, and may I never exchange it for a lie (Rom. 1:25). Reveal the lies I've believed for so long. Help me recognize them and replace them with Your truth. Lord, set me free.

Day 5- Father, may Your Holy Word never be choked out by the worries of this life, the deceitfulness of wealth, or desires for other things, (Mark 4:19). Give me a desire to spend more time with You in Your Word than with the distractions of this life. Help me read and study Your Word, growing closer to You, the Author, rather than just rely on Christian books and other sources.

Day 6- Lord, Your Word tells me I will have trouble in this world, but You also assure me that I don't have to live in defeat. In You, I can have peace and victory. Help me turn to You first and be filled with Your strength. Help me live with Your power. No matter my struggle, help me remember that You have overcome the world, that You love me, and in You, I am more than a conqueror! (John 16:33; Romans 8:37)

Day 7- Father, thank You for the faith You have given me. Before this faith came, I was held prisoner by the law, locked up until faith was revealed. (Gal. 3:23) But now Lord, in You, I am a new creation. The old has gone and I am free. Help me walk in this freedom every day with renewed strength and joy. (2 Cor. 5:17)

Day 8- Lord, according to Your Holy Word, my faith in You and my belief that Jesus is the Son of God gives me victory over the world. (I John 5:4-5) Help me believe You and let me see that faith is crucial if I am going to be a victor and an overcomer. Lord, please increase my faith in You and help my unbelief. (Mark 9:24)

Day 9- Father, I acknowledge that at times in my life I have fed on ashes instead of Your Word. I have let my misguided heart lead me astray. Help me recognize when I am holding onto a lie and trusting a powerless idol for my security, (Isaiah 44:20). Teach me to walk in Your truth and to completely trust in You alone.

Day 10- LORD, I praise You and magnify Your powerful name! Your Word is alive, powerful, and active. Sharper than any double-edged sword, it penetrates even to dividing soul and spirit, joints and marrow; it judges the thoughts and attitudes of the heart. Nothing in all creation is hidden from Your sight. Everything is uncovered and laid bare before You. Your Word exposes me for who I really am. (Heb. 4:12-13) Transform me, Lord. Create in me a clean heart, and renew a steadfast spirit within me, (Psalm 51:10).

Day 11- O Lord, please forgive me for my doubts. You are greater than my insecurities, and stronger than my fears. Help me to praise You because I am fearfully and wonderfully made; Your works are wonderful, I know that full well, (Psalm 139:14). Help me trust You completely as I will walk in Your freedom, (Psalm 119:45).

Day 12 - Lord, help me set my mind on things above, not on earthly things. (Col. 3:2) Help me allow Your Spirit to teach me to separate the temporary from the eternal and to set my focus on You (2 Cor. 4:18).

Day 13- Search my heart and mind, O God. Know my heart; test me and know my anxious thoughts. Lord, find every offensive way in me, and replace it with Your Truth. Lead me in the way everlasting (Ps. 139:23-24) and walking in Your freedom.

Day 14- Lord Jesus, You are alive! Thank You for conquering death and saving me. The same power that raised You from the dead lives in me. (Rom. 8:11) Fill me with Your Holy Spirit Lord and teach me to walk in Your ways. Your grace is sufficient and in my weakness You are strong. O Lord, may Your power rest in me! (2 Cor. 12:9)

Day 15- Father, even Jesus prayed to You for help while He lived on earth. He spent quiet time with You and prayed with loud cries and tears. (Heb. 5:7) Teach me to pray and seek You for help. Teach me to lean on Your strength and power. Lord, help me to pray, hear my prayers, and teach me to trust You completely.

Day 16- Father, You resist the proud but give grace to the humble. Help me clothe myself with humility toward others (1 Pet. 5:5), considering others above myself, (Phil. 2:3). I need Your grace every moment of every day. Protect me from every form of pride and help me maintain a humble, compassionate heart.

Day 17- Lord, God, You are my first desire and worthy of all praise. In all I do and say, help me make healthy, wholesome choices that honor You and bring You glory, (Col. 3:17). Free me from bondage to any questionable habits or hobbies. May I never allow worldly things to have control over me (1 Cor. 6:12). Rather, I choose to submit to You alone and experience freedom as I am guided and led by Your Spirit, (Gal. 5:18).

Day 18- Lord, You are my God who strengthens me, helps me, and upholds me in victory, power, and salvation. (Isaiah 41:10). Teach me to listen to You and accept Your perfect love. Help me have Your great joy. You are the only God, the One who saves me. To You be glory, greatness, power, and authority through Jesus Christ our Lord for all time past, present, and forever. Amen (Jude 24-25)

Day 19- Lord Jesus, You love me and have set me free, (Rom. 8:2). Reveal the lies I'm holding onto. Help me let go of the sin that so easily entangles me and holds me captive. Keep my focus on You, the author and perfecter of my faith (Heb. 12:2), the lifter of my head, and the One who has made me free.

Day 20- Lord, help me overcome my pride. Help me be full of Your Spirit and not full of myself. Enable me to humble myself under Your mighty hand so You can lift me up in due time (I Pet. 5:6) You are always trustworthy, and Your timing is always right. Help me to humble myself now so that You are free to do wonders later.

Day 21- Father God, make me strong and courageous. Help me never be afraid or intimidated because of anyone else. Help me live to please You rather than seeking the praises of men. For You, the Lord my God, are always with me. You will never leave me or forsake me. (Deut. 31:6)

Day 22 - Lord, my Holy One, my Creator, my King. You are the One who made a way through the sea, a path through the mighty waters. (Isa. 43:15-16) You alone are the Lord my God. Lord, I desire to love You. Help me listen to Your voice, and hold fast to You, for You, Lord, are my life, (Deut. 30:20), and in You, I am free.

Day 23- Lord, You proclaim freedom for the captives. (Isaiah 61:1) I belong to You and I am no longer a slave to this world or it's fears- I am free! Help me to live in Your freedom daily and look to You for my confidence and strength.

Day 24- Lord, I need You and desire to Know You more. Remove every sinful thought, and create in me a pure heart and a steadfast spirit, (Ps. 51:10-12). The old is gone. Help me let go of shame, regret, and every sin, that I may live in Your freedom, as You desire for me. I am a brand new creation and I praise You! (Gal. 5:17).

Day 25- Lord, I believe Your Word, Your promises, and I need Your strength. I pray that You, the God of hope, will fill me with all joy and peace as I trust You. Help me abound in hope by the power of Your Holy Spirit (Rom. 15:13).

Day 26- Father, teach me to abide in You and trust You completely. Strengthen me that I might never be taken captive by lies or philosophies of this world, or rely on human tradition (Col. 2:8) Help me trust completely in Your great strength, rely on Your Word above all else, and live by Your truth.

Day 27- Dear God, no matter what I once was, I have been washed, I have been sanctified, and I have been justified in the name of the Lord Jesus Christ and by the Spirit of our God, (1 Cor. 6:11). I am clean, and I am free! Lord God, help me fully accept how much You love me, and help me abide in Your freedom and love (John 15:9).

Day 28- Lord, teach me to turn all my worries and cares over to You, (1 Peter 5:7). Remove every fear, anxiety, and sinful desire, and fill me with Your peace beyond what I can comprehend. Guard my heart and my mind in Christ Jesus (Phil. 4:5-7) and help me abide in Your love and grace.

Day 29 - You, O Lord, are my rock, my refuge, my stronghold, and my deliverer! (2 Samuel 22:2). Remove every evil thing I have exalted above You and help me rest in the knowledge that You and You alone are my greatest stronghold! I am not held captive any longer. In Christ, I am free. In my freedom, help me make choices that bring You glory, Lord, and which bring me closer to You. Increase my knowledge of You and my desire to walk in Your freedom!

Day 30- Almighty God, help me no longer conform to the pattern of this world, but transform me by the renewing of my mind. Lord, help me place my life before You as an offering. Change me from the inside out. Help me stand firm against the sins of the culture, and help me look like Jesus as You develop well-formed maturity in me (Romans 12:1-2).

Day 31- Father, Your Word says it is for freedom that Christ has set me free. With all my heart, I desire to stand firm and never again allow myself to be burdened by a yoke of slavery (Gal. 5:1). I surrender and submit to You completely, and rest in Your goodness and strength. I acknowledge my weakness and rejoice because I know that Your power is made perfect in my weakness (2 Cor. 12:9-10). Strengthen me to walk in the freedom You have already given me. Teach me to stand firm. I can do all things in Christ who strengthens me! (Phil. 4:13)

Made in United States
North Haven, CT
31 July 2022